From Zero To One Million Followers

Followers

How To Build A Massive Following
In One Month As A Influencer

By

Sandra Jakes

electronic or mechanical methods.

TABLE OF CONTENT

Chapter 6: Growth Hacks

Chapter 7: Monetization And Beyond

Conclusion

Introduction

In the vast digital environment of the 21st century, a new kind of dream has emerged: a dream without limits of influence, creativity and communication.

This is a dream that lives at the heart of social media, where people from all walks of life are rising from obscurity to become digital experts, working to inspire and engage an audience of millions.

Welcome to the journey from zero to one million followers. This ebook is your guide and navigator through the fascinating and complex world of social media influence.

Whether you're an aspiring content creator, a seasoned entrepreneur, or just looking to amplify your voice, From Zero to a Million Followers is an exciting adventure you're invited to join.

The next chapter explores the complex and innovative

process of building a large online readership.

We'll guide you step by step, from finding your niche to developing your brand, from creating compelling content to engaging your audience, from hacking to growth and monetization.

This journey isn't just about crunching the numbers.

It's about making meaningful connections, creating great content, and making an impact.

It's about learning the skills to make an impact while staying true to your unique voice and values.

The digital frontier is constantly changing, offering unprecedented opportunities to those who want to dream, create and connect.

Using this ebook as your compass, you'll want to embark on a transformative adventure to discover the secrets, strategies, and insights that can take you from zero to a million followers.

Are you ready to take the first step towards your digital future? The road is open, adventure awaits, and the world is ready to change.

Let's go from 0 to 1 million subscribers together.

Chapter 1
The Power Of Mass Construction

In the age of social media, influence is its own currency. The ability to reach, engage and impact the lives of millions has become an ambition for many.

Whether you're an aspiring content creator, an entrepreneur, or just someone who likes to share their passion, the appeal of building a large online following is undeniable.

This eBook will guide you on your journey to grow from zero followers to a million followers in just one month.

Impact Occurrence

Social media has revolutionized the way we communicate, connect and consume content.
Platforms like Instagram, TikTok, YouTube and Twitter have leveled the playing field, allowing people with unique voices and stories to amass enough followers to compete with celebrities and large corporations.

This democratization of influence is a double-edged sword.

It presents an unprecedented opportunity for anyone with a compelling message or niche, but it also creates enormous challenges in a sea of creators trying to get noticed.

Why it's important to find a great following

You might be wondering:
Why is it so important to
build a large following?
The answers vary.

Having a significant
following isn't just about
empty stats or bragging
rights.
This provides real benefits.

Influence: The more
followers you have, the
greater your reach and
influence.
You can impact more lives,
raise awareness about

issues you care about, and create real change.

Monetization: Having a significant number of followers opens up more monetization opportunities.
Brands are looking for influencers to promote their products or services, and you can turn your passion into a rewarding career.

Personal branding: Building a following isn't just about the numbers.

It's about building a unique personal brand.

Your online presence builds your reputation, opens the door to exciting collaborations, and offers opportunities that are sure to fit your niche.

Network and Connect: We help many of our listeners connect with like-minded industry experts and people. It gives you a platform to connect and collaborate with others who share your interests.

Fulfillment: It can be satisfying to know that your content is resonating with a large audience.
Sharing your creativity or experience with millions of people can be a rewarding endeavor.

Set realistic expectations

The promise of going from zero to a million followers in a month is tempting, but it's important to approach the journey with authenticity. Building a large following, especially in a short period of time, is not an easy task and requires hard work, creativity and strategy.

Designed to provide step-by-step guidance, this e-book offers insights, strategies, and tactics to help you achieve these ambitious goals.

Before embarking on this exciting journey, it is very important to understand that there are no guarantees in the world of social media.

Success depends on many factors, including your niche, the quality of your content, and consistent communication with your audience.

Some people experience rapid growth, while others may take longer to reach their goals.

The key is to be persistent, adapt to change and continually improve your approach.

Remember, the journey to a million followers is as much about self-awareness and personal growth as it is about gaining followers.

Becoming an influencer is a transformational process that gives you skills, knowledge and experience that go beyond your social media profiles.

Chapter 2
Finding A Niche

In a digital world where so many voices are competing for attention, finding your niche is like finding a secret weapon.

Your niche is a unique area, a specific subject, or a topic that you are passionate about and know about.

This is the cornerstone of your journey from obscurity to internet fame.

Why niches matter

Think of social media as a huge market with countless stalls selling different products. To stand out in this crowded market, you need a stand that is unique and offers what people want.

This is your place.

Passion and Authenticity: Choosing a niche that you are truly passionate about makes it easier to create content, connect with your audience, and maintain your passion over time. Authenticity resonates with your followers and is key to building trust.

Target Audience: Specific niches allow you to target a specific audience that is interested in that topic. They are the most receptive to your content.

Less competition: Narrowing your focus can lead to less competition than if you tried to cover a wider range of topics.

Experience and Credibility: Gaining knowledge and experience in your niche can help you position yourself as an authority. Credibility increases your appeal to both your audience and potential employees.

Discover your niche

Identify your passion: Take the time to think of something you love and can talk about endlessly.
Your passion is a source of inspiration and motivation in your journey.

Market Research: Find out what's happening in your area of interest.
Find out what's popular, what's trending, and what gaps or underserved areas exist.

Target group analysis: Think about who you want to reach.

What are their interests, problems and needs?

Your niche should match the needs of your target audience.

Originality: Find out what makes you unique in your chosen niche.

Your personal experiences, perspectives or new perspectives can make you stand out.

Balance between passion and demand

Passion is important, but so is finding a balance between what you like and what you want.

This is a two-part equation.

Your passion matches what you are passionate about and there is an audience interested in that niche.

Passion-based: A niche that matches your passion

motivates you, but also ensures that there is an audience for it.

Determined Demand: A high-demand niche can be tempting, but it's important to have a genuine interest in the subject to sustain your efforts.

Research: If you're not sure about your niche, experiment.

Try different topics and see what resonates with your audience and personal passions.

Cases and examples

Looking at real-life examples of successful influencers can be enlightening.
For example, someone who loves to travel might specialize in off-road destinations, while someone who loves fitness

might focus on home workouts for busy parents.

Remember, your niche is not set in stone.

As you grow and develop as an influencer, your niche can grow as well. The key is to stay true to your interests and the needs of your audience while adapting to changing trends and opportunities.

Once you've found your niche, you're ready to move on to the next step in your journey: building your brand, creating engaging content, and engaging your audience.

Your niche is your foundation and gives you clear direction as you work to reach millions of followers.

Chapter 3
Building Your Brand

Your brand is more than just a logo, a color scheme or a clever slogan.

It is the essence of your online presence, the promise you make to your followers and their perception of you.

Building a strong brand is essential to building a large following as it helps you stand out in a crowded digital environment and builds awareness and trust with your audience.

The components of a brand

Identity: This includes your name, profile picture and username. Your name should reflect your niche and your profile picture should be clear, professional and relevant to your niche.

Voice: Your brand voice is how you communicate with your audience.
Is it informal, informative and humorous?

Your pitch should fit your niche and resonate with your target audience.

Values: Your brand values should reflect your personal beliefs and the topics you promote in your niche.
Consistency in values helps build trust.

Visuals: Consistent visuals such as colors, fonts and image styles create a brand that stands out.

This should be reflected in your profile, messaging and promotional materials.

Story: Your brand story is the story that ties everything together.
Share your journey, why you are starting your niche and your goals as an influencer.

Brand definition

Self-reflection: Think about who you are and what you want to represent.
Think about your passions, beliefs and what makes you unique.

Niche Alignment: Make sure your brand fits your niche.
Your brand should convey what you stand for and what your audience expects from you.

Consider your audience: Think about what will resonate with your target audience.

What do people find attractive, popular and valuable about your brand?

Brand consistency

Consistency is the foundation of brand building.

Your followers need to know what to expect from you.

People who see your posts on social media, your website or other platforms should immediately recognize your brand.

Content Consistency: Maintain a consistent style in your posts, regardless of the type of content you create (eg tutorials, reviews, vlogs) or the structure of your content (eg captions, video intros).

Visual Consistency: Use the same colors, fonts and

design elements across all brand materials.This promotes awareness.

Tonal Consistency: Make sure your voice and message are aligned with your brand values and niche.

Building trust through branding

Your brand is a tool for building trust. Trust is very important in the influencer space because it determines whether people will follow you, engage with your content, or buy based on your recommendations.

Transparency: Be open and honest with your audience. Transparency helps build trust by showing that you are honest and not hiding anything.

Consistency: We've discussed content consistency, but it's important to remember that trust and consistency in your publishing table builds trust.

Provide value: Make sure your content consistently provides value to your audience.Whether it's in the form of entertainment, education, inspiration, or any other value, it's important to deliver on your promises.

Cases and examples

Let's take the example of a fitness influencer who runs a brand that aims to promote a healthy lifestyle.

Their brand identity includes a sleek logo, vivid imagery and consistent messaging about the benefits of exercise and nutrition.

Their voice is upbeat and encouraging and reflects their values of health and wellness.

Building a brand is an ongoing process.

As you grow and learn more about your audience and niche, your brand can evolve.

The key is to stay authentic, stay true to your values, and keep your audience's needs and expectations at the forefront of your branding efforts.

Having a strong and consistent brand will leave you better equipped to move forward and create content that resonates with your audience, ultimately helping you grow from zero to a million followers.

Chapter 4
Content Creation

Content creation is the engine that fuels your journey to build a large following. Your content is the bridge that connects you to your audience, communicates your message and, when executed effectively, turns casual viewers into loyal followers.

This chapter takes a closer look at the art and science of creating engaging content.

The importance of engaging content

Creating engaging content isn't just about sharing what you love.

It's about creating content that resonates with your target audience and keeps them coming back for more.

Here's what to keep in mind:

Relevance: Your content should be relevant to your niche and brand.

It must be valuable and relevant to your audience's interests and needs.

Quality: High-quality content stands out. Invest in good photo and video equipment and take the time to edit and improve your work.

Originality: While it's common to take inspiration from others, you should try to bring a unique style and perspective to your content.It makes you stand out.

Consistency: Maintain a consistent posting schedule.Regular content engages your audience and demonstrates your commitment.

Choose the right content type

The right content format depends on your niche,

audience preferences and strengths.

Common types of content include:

Photography and Graphics: Ideal for visually appealing niches such as fashion, travel and food.

High quality images are essential.

Video: From short clips to long-form content, video can effectively capture your audience's attention. Platforms like YouTube, TikTok and Instagram Reels are ideal for video content.

Written content: Blog posts, headlines and articles can be very informative and engaging.

Live Stream: Real-time audience interaction can be exciting and authentic.

Infographics: Ideal for simplifying complex information or statistics.

Content strategy and planning

A strategic approach to content creation is essential for continued growth.

Consider the following steps:

Content Calendar: Plan your content in advance. A content calendar helps you stay organized and maintain a consistent posting schedule.

Mix up your content: Diversify your content to keep it fresh.
A combination of educational, inspirational and entertaining content can help you capture the attention of your audience.

Storytelling: Add engaging stories to your content. Stories are more relevant and memorable than simple information.

Engagement Strategy: Think about how your content encourages engagement. Asking questions, taking surveys, and asking for feedback promote interaction.

Visual and aesthetic appeal

The visual aspect of your content is important.
Imagine the following situation:

Photography Skills: If your niche involves visual content, take the time to improve your photography skills.

Editing tools: Learn how to effectively edit photos and videos. Tools like Adobe

Lightroom and Canva can help.

Consistent   Aesthetics:
Maintain   a   consistent
visual   style,   including
colors, filters, and overall
look.
Sustainable aesthetics are
becoming more and more
recognized.

quality   and   quantity :
Finding the right balance is
important.High-quality

content is essential to engage your audience and attract new subscribers.But consistency is also important.

It's often better to consistently create high-quality content than to create the occasional masterpiece.Analyze and learn from your audience

Pay attention to reviews and feedback.

Platforms often provide insight into what works

and what doesn't. Use this information to adjust your content strategy.

Adaptation and Evolution

The digital environment is constantly changing. Be prepared to adapt to new trends and technologies. Experiment with different content formats and be open to innovation.

Cases and examples

Think of a lifestyle influencer in your fitness niche.

They create mixed content that includes educational videos, recipe tutorials, and motivational posts.

Their content matches their style, with vivid visuals and a clear, strong brand voice.

This variety and consistency allows you to maintain interest by catering to different aspects of your audience's interests.

Creating compelling content is an ongoing process, an art refined through experience. Capturing your audience's attention and turning them into loyal supporters is an essential part of getting from 0 to 1 million followers.

Chapter 5
Engaging Your Audience

Audience engagement is an essential step in taking your followers from zero to a million. A highly engaged audience engages with your content and becomes loyal followers.

This chapter details strategies and tactics for actively engaging your audience in your online journey.

Why engaging your audience is important

Engagement is the lifeblood of your online presence.

It's not just about the number of followers.

It's about the depth of connection you have with them.

Your target followers may:

Be proactive.

They will continue to engage with your content and increase your visibility.

Promote yourself: They will share your content and recommend you to their friends.

Trust yourself: Highly engaged people trust your recommendations and are more likely to engage with your sponsored content.
Give feedback: This will give you valuable insight into what's working and what's not.

Develop an engagement strategy

Content that encourages interaction: Create content that encourages your audience to comment, share or tag others.
This can be done through questions, surveys, quizzes or calls to action.

Respond to comments: Connect with your audience by responding to comments on your posts.

By acknowledging their comments and questions, you show that you value their opinions.

Storytelling: Share personal stories and experiences that your audience can relate to.Authenticity is an important factor in engagement.

Polls and questions: Encourage participation in the conversation using interactive features like polls, questions, and quizzes.

Live Interaction: Host a live stream or Q&A session to engage with your audience in real time.Direct interaction is often very engaging.

Building a community
Try to create a sense of community among your followers.
Encourage interaction with others as well as yourself.

Consider these community building strategies:

Create a Hashtag: Create a unique hashtag for your community.

Create a shared ID and encourage your followers to use it.

User Generated Content: Includes content created by your followers.This not only recognizes their contributions but also creates a sense of belonging.

Join the conversation: Start discussions and conversations related to your niche.Invite your audience to share their opinions and experiences.

Consistency and commitment

Consistency in engagement is just as important as consistency in posting content.Get into the habit of responding quickly to comments, messages and emails. This shows that you value your audience's time and opinions.

Dealing with negative feedback

Negative reviews are inevitable.
Be kind to them:

Act professionally. Respond professionally and avoid heated discussions.

Use constructive feedback: If the criticism is constructive, use it as an opportunity to improve.

Set boundaries: It's important to set boundaries and remove or block people who are harmful or rude.

cheers and cheers
Collaboration with others increases engagement. Collaborations and promotions can introduce your content to new

audiences and strengthen existing relationships.

Growth participation hacking

Growth hacks like contests, giveaways, or themed challenges will quickly increase engagement. These strategies often create a sense of urgency and excitement among audiences.

stability and patience

Building an engaged audience takes time.

Be consistent in your engagement efforts and don't get discouraged by slow growth.

Over time, your dedication to maintaining relationships with your followers will pay off.

Cases and examples

Consider a beauty influencer who regularly interacts with her followers.She encourages people to share her makeup looks using her unique hashtag and frequently posts her work on her page. By creating a community where writers can showcase their talents and be inspired by each other, we've not only increased engagement, but also built a loyal and supportive following.

Audience engagement is an ongoing effort that can go a

long way in your journey from zero to a million followers.

As you continue to create content and engage with your followers, you'll find that your engaged audience will share your content and help you reach new goals.

Chapter 6
Growth Hacks

Growth Hacking is the art of finding unconventional, creative and fast ways to grow your online following. As you grow from zero to a million followers, growth hacking becomes a valuable strategy to accelerate your journey.

This chapter explores various tactics and strategies to encourage growth.

Use hashtags

Hashtags help you reach a wider audience.
Use them strategically to increase your income.

Research:

Identify popular and relevant hashtags in your niche.Tools like Instagram's search function and hashtag generator can help.

Variety:

Use a mix of popular, specific and niche hashtags.The latter allows you to reach a more involved target group.

Branded Hashtag:
Create a unique branded hashtag that fits your niche or content.Create a sense of community and encourage your followers to use it.

Trending Hashtags:
Identify popular or seasonal hashtags and join the conversations around them.

Analysis and statistics

Many social media platforms offer analytics and insights into your performance.

To use these tools:

Track your progress: track subscriber growth, post reach and other important metrics.

Audience Insights: Understand your audience's demographics and preferences to personalize your content.

Best times to post: Determine when your audience is most active and schedule your posts accordingly.

cheers and cheers
Collaborating with others in your niche can expand your reach exponentially.

Collaborate with influencers: Collaborate with influencers who share your target audience.Crossmouter can expose your content to a whole new group of potential followers.

Announcement: Tell other authors and they may respond. This mutually beneficial experience helps both parties grow.

Addressing trends and challenges

Responding to trends and challenges on social media platforms can expose your content to a wider audience.

Be active: participate in testing trends and use relevant hashtags to increase your visibility.

Create Your Own Challenge: Start your own challenge or trend in your niche.
If you catch it, it can go viral.

viral strategy
Going viral is every content creator's dream. While you can't predict, there are strategies that can increase your chances.

Emotional content: Content that evokes strong emotions (laughter, inspiration, empathy, etc.) is more likely to go viral.

Shareable content: Create shareable content. Memes, infographics and short videos are very common.

Capitalize on trends: Take advantage of popular topics, but add your own unique twist or perspective.

Earn money with advertising

Consider investing some of your revenue from influencer partnerships or sponsorships to promote your content.

Paid Advertising: Reach a wider audience using paid advertising on platforms like Facebook and Instagram.

Promoted Posts: Reach a wider audience by promoting your most popular or engaging posts.

community involvement

Don't forget your existing followers.They can be your most influential promoters.

Encourage sharing: Encourage your followers to share your content and invite their friends to follow you.

Run Contests: Run contests and giveaways that require

followers, such as tagging friends and sharing content.

Ask for referrals: If your audience finds your content valuable, ask them directly to recommend your network.
adaptation and development

Growth Hacking is about discovering what works for you.

Be prepared to adjust and evolve your strategy as you determine what works best for your audience.

Cases and examples

Consider a fitness content creator.They found that certain fitness issues were trending in the wider fitness community.

They decided to get involved, document their progress and share their unique journey.

By using popular challenge hashtags, you gain

visibility among a large and engaged audience and significantly increase your followers.

Growth Hacking is the art of experimentation.
It's about discovering what resonates with your audience, taking calculated risks and continually improving your approach.
By implementing these strategies, you will be equipped to accelerate your journey to gaining millions of followers.

Chapter 7
Monetization And Beyond

Reaching 1 million followers is a significant achievement and opens up a world of opportunities for further monetization and growth.
In this chapter, we'll look at how you can connect with your audience and use your influence for success and growth.

Monetization options

Sponsorships: Partnerships with brands that fit your niche.
Sponsored posts, product reviews, and compliments can help.

Affiliate Marketing: Promote your product or service and earn a commission for every sale made through your unique affiliate link.

Sell Products: If you've developed a product, such

as merchandise or a digital product (e.g. eBook, course), promote and sell it to your followers.

Online Courses and Workshops: Share your expertise by offering online courses or workshops.Platforms such as Udemy, Teachable or Skillshare may be suitable for hosting courses.

Ads and ad networks: Once you have enough subscribers, you can start earning money by displaying ads. Platforms like Google AdSense and the YouTube Affiliate Program offer this option.

Consulting and Coaching: If you have expertise in a niche, offer consulting or coaching services to your followers.

Subscription or subscription model: Platforms like Patreon

allow you to encourage your most loyal subscribers to support a monthly subscription and offer them exclusive content or benefits in return.

Diversify your income streams

Consider diversifying your income sources to protect your financial stability. Relying on a single source can be risky.

Stay honest

Don't compromise authenticity when it comes to making money. Your audience will follow you because they resonate with your content and trust your recommendations.

Promote products or services you truly believe in.

Consistency and commitment

Making money doesn't mean you have to stop

communicating with your audience.

In fact, it is very important to maintain a strong relationship with your followers because an engaged audience is more likely to support your project.

strategic expansion

Once you have over 1 million followers, consider expanding strategically.

New Platforms: Explore new social media platforms or expand your presence on existing platforms. Diversifying your online presence will help you reach a wider audience.

Collaborate: Continue to collaborate with influencers in your niche or neighboring niches. Collaboration helps you find new networks and followers.

Cross-promote: Once you've developed a product or service, try partnering with other influencers to cross-promote it. Their audience can become a valuable customer base.

Professional Development: Invest in personal growth and professional development.
Keep learning and improving your content creation and marketing skills.

Delegation and scaling: As your workload increases, consider hiring a team to handle aspects of your impact activities, such as content creation, marketing and business management.
long term branding

Remember that your influence journey is a long-term endeavor.

Focus on building a strong, sustainable personal brand that transcends passing trends.

Think about how you can add value to your audience over the years.

Cases and examples

Imagine a traveler reaching a million followers.They decided to monetize their platform by partnering with travel agents for sponsored trips, generating revenue through affiliate marketing through hotel bookings, and creating a line of travel accessories.

We offer exclusive travel tips and guides and even launch online courses for our followers.

This influencer has successfully diversified his income while staying true to his niche.

Monetization and scaling are exciting steps in an influencer's journey.

The road from zero to a million is a tough one, but here are the next steps you can take to turn your passion into a sustainable career.

By staying authentic, connecting with your audience, and strategically expanding your influence, you can realize your potential for successful influence.

Conclusion

Your journey from zero to a million followers has set you on a unique adventure.

You've navigated the digital landscape, overcome challenges and harnessed the power of social media to build an incredible following.

But this journey is not just about numbers.

This is a testament to your dedication, creativity and resilience.

I've learned that success as an influencer isn't just about where you go, it's also about the path you take.

It's about the stories you share, the connections you make and the community you build. The value you provide to your audience is immeasurable, and the trust they place in you is priceless.

As we conclude this e-book, it is important to remember that influence is an ongoing effort. Your journey is a continuous cycle of innovation, improvement and reinvention.

Getting 0-1 million followers may not be the same as getting 1-10 million followers.

Staying authentic, engaging your audience and staying true to your values will be your guiding principles.

The brand you carefully build remains your

compass in a dynamic digital environment.

In the next chapter of your influencer story, you'll monetize your reach and grow your influence as you continue to inspire, educate, and entertain your growing audience.

As you reach new heights, remember that the journey is just as important as the destination.

Embrace challenges, learn from failures and celebrate milestones.
Because it's all part of the impact journey.

Whether you have a million followers, over a million followers, or just getting started, the path ahead is full of potential.
With the skills and knowledge you gain from this eBook, you'll be better equipped to navigate the complex and ever-evolving

world of social media influence.

So, move forward into the future with confidence.
Because it's not just about building a following.
You are building a legacy.
Your impact will continue to impact lives, spark conversations and create change.
You have the power to inspire and that's what makes your journey from zero to a million followers so special.